Cover art and illustrations by :
Ysabelle Jao

Trigger warning
The contents of this poetry collection involves mentions of
trauma, sexual abuse, depression, disordered eating, and
graphic topics/imagery. Please take precautions reading
ahead.

Samaritans helpline
116 123

Contents

THE GIFT OF

IMPERMANENCE

By

Bernadette Millan

*Welcome to a journey
that will never really finish.*

Bernadette Millan

My past has not been kind to my heart.
It may take forever for my soul to be cured.

Dear future me,
Please be patient.

It haunts me
the way that this youth
is filled with fragmented souls,
yet have hearts filled with gold.
It is sad that so much hate
had silenced the mouths of those
who just want to love.
There is too much misery,
too much anger,
too much pain,
too little joy.

Bernadette Millan

Your unwanted mark on my skin,
felt like needles riding up the skirt that I wore.
I just wanted to feel beautiful.
Was this a side effect of me
just wanting to *feel* good enough?
Did I ask for this?
Did I have to bleed in order to be contented?
Is this what I desired?

Well, at least I'm wanted,
even if I didn't really want to be.

<u>Falling for a</u>
Falling in love with one that has no heart,
is like falling for an object,
an item,
a *thing*.
No matter how hard you really try,
it will never have any meaning.
At least not to them.
It is like screaming at a chair,
and showing your pain to it.
It won't do you any justice.
It won't feel any remorse.
It won't feel anything.
Absolute nothingness.

Bernadette Millan

I don't hate you,
if I did
it would be easier to accept the fact
that whilst my eyes build up an army of tears
that threaten to tumble down my face,
a smile slowly creeps up on yours.

The Gift of Impermanence

I wish there were more words and ways
to explain the emptiness
that gnaws at my chest.
A deafening quietude
that dawdles in the night time.
The pain that I am feeling
is more than my heart could bare,
it has drained me,
sucked all my puissance.
The moon fell sympathetic
as she saw unhappiness in my eyes,
thus bringing the stars out
and making them glisten against my skin
as well as for the stars and the wind
to act as her loving arms
so that she could cup my face
and wipe my tears away.

At night, I feel the least lonely.

Heal me with poison,
hold me with a dagger to my heart.
You make me insane,
yet keep me lucid.
I wish you weren't such a bad person.
Because it's too late now to get back the pieces of me
that I gave to you.

The Gift of Impermanence

Tragedy follows me around
like a lousy shadow.
An unwanted silhouette.
A mistaken outline.
It haunts me,
lurks within the corners of the room,
and suffocates me at night
with a pillow filled with loud memories.

Bernadette Millan

<u>Air.</u>
You pulsate my entire being,
drifting me into your blissful grasp.
Your lightweight arms swoop me in a cunning lullaby,
a peaceful howl.
You sweep away all the pain,
the suffering,
the agony,
with just the blow of your warm breath
the moment you open your mouth to speak,
replacing it with something so pure.

The Gift of Impermanence

Sadness is intimate with me.
We'd cuddle in bed most nights,
and have dinner together.
Some nights we're so close that we share the same plate.
One half for me, one half for them.
We'd go to stores together,
but they'd get angry when I'd talk to people,
so I tend to just look away.
Sadness says I look prettier when I don't brush my hair.
Sadness says I should stay in bed for *just* a few more hours.
We would shower together too,
they like it scolding hot,
hot enough to make me feel a burning nothing.

We do everything together,
It's all very romantic.

I wouldn't say I'm contented,
I'd say I'm just comfortable.

I have succumbed to the numbing feeling,
a fortress of limitless catastrophe.
Pure solitude lies on the bed in the forest
that I rest upon.
I have been swallowed whole
by eternal anguish.

The Gift of Impermanence

I

Permanence mocks us sometimes,
nothing really stays.
Like the happiness that made its way through your veins
is living on nothing but borrowed time.

Bernadette Millan

A flower can be so deadly,
though she is a seductress.
Her scent can hold you spellbound
whilst her thorns plunge in deeper
without you even noticing.
Be careful as you tread closer,
she can kill your soul
and convince you that you had asked for this.

I want to be happy someday.
I want to be happy and *not* afraid,
that with the presence of my happiness,
the world will make a cruel joke
and have the pillars I have built to collapse on me.

Bernadette Millan

The idea of pain excites me.
The thought of crawling inside someone else's skin
and dictating on how they feel is somewhat a thrill.

Maybe I could use ice
and freeze every speck of warmth that snuggles in the
chambers of their hearts.
Cold enough that they won't ever go back to the amiable
soul that they had.

Or maybe I could use fire
and burn each vein, each organ,
until their body fills up in flames,
with the only thing putting it out
is the sound of their cupboard door
and the popping sound of the whiskey glass
before guzzling it down like water.

I don't know what it is.
Maybe it's the power,
or maybe I just want someone else to fuel
in order for the bullet that's lodged into my chest
to hurt less,
even just a little bit,
knowing that somebody else is hurting too.

Behind every baby picture,
and pretty little memories,
I always think to myself
"At which point exactly did it all go wrong?"

Bernadette Millan

How does it feel
to swarm my mind?
Your face lurking in every crevice,
in every blank space.
How does it feel to be wanted
by *everyone*?

Does it make you feel good?

Does it make you any more heartless
than you already are?

How barbaric is it,
that the world provides us with things
out of our reach.
It is the chase for the unceasing paradise
that taunts us that we could never really,
truly,
be happy.

Do you feel like this sometimes?
I know I do.

I find it difficult
to accept the fact that
you will never be the person
that I envisioned.
I have given up on the presence of hope.
I shouldn't mix the existence of you,
with a person that is only alive in my head.

The Gift of Impermanence

Dear Dad,

Your faceless figure floats in my head,
like an unwanted feather.
The scent that you had left behind became dull,
unidentifiable,
along with the feeling of your embrace vanishing from my
memories.
Your eyes don't emerge in my mind anymore,
the color of your hair seemed to blur.
The image of you now unknown,
and I can't help but feel as though I am losing you
for the second time.

It hurts.
My body hurts.
The food has razors embedded into them
and they'll make me bleed with every bite I take.
At night I can hear my skin screaming.
They are weeping with anguish and disgust.

They don't want me to bleed anymore.

The Gift of Impermanence

My soul would melt
around the fire that's ignited
within the furnace upon your eyes,
warming me up until I'm the right temperature for you.
And you gulp me like wine
until there is none left
that you don't possess.

Is this what love feels like?

Bernadette Millan

The first

I was only young when I experienced the touch of love.
Whether it was real or not, it didn't really matter.
The stinging pain was an abyss of pulchritude,
the sounds of laughter did not content me.
Why must I love the feeling of agony to kiss my neck,
my lips, my eyes that is already filled with fog?
I asked myself that every night after the presence of a door
slamming.
The voice of the oak wood colliding sent nothing but
comfort.
Surely, I asked myself, *Love is supposed to hurt.*
Surely, I asked myself, *I wanted this.*
Dolos' eyes enchanted me, the firmament wept,
I swooped into the arms of a lost soul in shining armour.
With every argument, thunderstorms of malefic rage
cracked the walls and shattered the grounds of the Earth
until my voice became impuissant.

I left that love.

I left a part of me. A part of me that had turned mute.
However I was only young when I experienced the hold of
cupid.
Whether it was real or not, it did not matter one bit.

It is hard to live in the present day
when my past has a way
of *keeping me quiet.*

Grief can be humorous at times.
It creeps up when you are on an uphill climb
furthering the progress towards recovery,
with the gift of your heart hurting a little less.
What a funny, peculiar way
for Grief to make sure that we have not forgotten
about its principles.
To think that the companionship of it
could spew out randomly
from within the interstices of
a dam that is built by a soul
that attempts to move on.
It can happen so suddenly,
as if a warning is unfamiliar
with regards to its welcoming.
And you have nothing else to do
but to accept it's attendance with open arms,
else it would threaten the ocean of tears
to pool out from your enervated eyes.

The Gift of Impermanence

When your lips collide with mine,
it is like strolling through a field that has
an abundance of yellow irises;
a melody strings out;
a harp plays with every peck you plant.
The sun grins wide and full
and the water droplets flirt
until they spew out from the clouds above,
making it rain over us,
with each droplet nudging us closer together
until our lips meet again.

I was eight years old when I moved to England.
It was all exciting until two boys in my class started calling
me an "*alien*" because I was from another country.
I remember not thinking too much into it.
That is until the whole class started to laugh and chant with
them,
"She's an alien!".

It's funny how something like that could affect the way I
saw myself. I remember all the way throughout my primary
school years, I'd hide my lunch because of what my mother
cooked. I remember hating my eyes, how big my lips were
compared to my classmates, and how I could understand
another language other than English. It's *sad*.

It gets difficult at times, trying to undo the detestation I had
towards where I came from. But I hope you can forgive me.

*I still catch myself apologising to people if the house
smells.*

Her tears water
the blooming dandelions
as they mature into adulthood.
She was their mother now.
And with sympathy,
these dandelions gave themselves to her
so that she could make wishes
to cure her heartache.

Bernadette Millan

I would give up everything
to be able to come home
and smell the nostalgic scent that lingers within the walls of
the kitchen.
To be able to feel the embrace that loiter
between you and I.
It is as if when you left,
your soul rested its weight on my back,
because why does everything else feel heavier to do now?

I wish that time did not have to mock us,
I hope that it felt bad.
Bad enough to slow down for me,
because it's been years now,
yet a teardrop is still not ripe enough
to fall down my face.

To those who are mourning.

The Gift of Impermanence

Green is my favourite colour.
Green is Nature's essence, it's innate lipstick.
I wear green sometimes,
only when I'm happy.
I wear green when I dance with flowers,
I wear green when I want the clouds to notice me,
I wear green when I flirt with the sun
as it plants its lips across my cheeks.
I never used to like green that much.
I used to have yellow wrapped around me,
a bright yellow,
brighter than a fresh-born sunflower.
And then you walked in,
your silhouette shone the perfect shade of blue.
And when our paths slowly became one,
we created an endless garden of emeralds.

Half of my heart is ancient,
a fragile crooked glass,
it could break any second
yet I'd still give it to you.

The Gift of Impermanence

Dear Mama,
Sometimes I do not understand you. Sometimes I do not
understand the way you get angry at certain things,
or when you get stressed if I accidentally leave the fridge
slightly ajar.
Maybe it's just how you grew up to be.
Maybe it's just how you are.
I spent nights getting frustrated after we'd have petty fights
over the unwashed dishes in the kitchen sink,
or how late I stayed out at night when I was just 15 years
old.
I didn't notice it then,
but I do now.
It hurts when I stay out late and see my phone,
you being absent.
It hurts when I'd be the first one throughout the day to call
or text a *'good morning'* or a *'how are you?'*.
It hurts to acknowledge, finally, that I pushed you away,
to a point where you couldn't even reach me with your
fingertips.
It hurts to know that I'd provided miles to rest between us
when we were in the same room, mere inches away from
each other.
It hurts to know that I grew up without you,
because I know that it would've meant the world
to raise me like a mother you've always wanted to be.
But I didn't let you then.
And now,
you will forever feel a failure,
when it wasn't even your fault.
I'm sorry, Mama.

Our paths will always
inevitably cross each other.
Your eyes, my love,
they could never meet mine.
They could never meet in the way I want them to.
I know because the glow that took shelter
within my gaze shone bright enough
that it disregarded the dimness in yours.
I fell for that artificial smile
that you had plastered out of pity,
with me hoping that a glimpse of it were
even the tiniest bit genuine.
Your laugh was a hoax,
along with the tenderness of your touch
that you had secretly saved for somebody else.
Somebody that was not me.
I cannot force you to love me,
I cannot force you to want me,
to need me the way that I need you.
I just wish that I wouldn't feel this bad
for loving you so much
that it makes me loathe you for not feeling the same.

The Gift of Impermanence

The deafening screams that are entrapped
through the sobs and agony,
that then remains within the skin of my pillows.
It rests on the bed my body engraved a perpetual dimple
on.

My room does not feel like a home anymore.
It has become a constant reminder
of the desolation I endured.

We now live in a world where a mistake,
has the power to hold people on leashes.
We now live in a flawed world where
it has to be perfect,
or it all just falls apart.
That just doesn't seem fair.

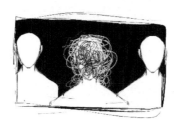

II

I can cope with the temporary fix,
but Happiness has gone through everybody already,
it's not come back to me yet.
So tell me,
When is it *my* turn again?

Bernadette Millan

The beguiling voices of the sirens
would appear lurking within your shadows.
Your tongue dipped with a love potion,
your mouth intertwined with the veins of Aphrodite.
It is with agonising pleasure,
to be held under your trance.

The Gift of Impermanence

Rowena

Don't stay out after dark.
She said as she fumbled with the ironing board,
making sure that my clothes remained pristine.

Make sure you eat all your vegetables.
The scraping of the metal fork became audible,
as her warm hands urged the lump of carrots
I had built on the side of my plate to approach me.

Make sure you sleep.
As she traced her fingertips on my forehead,
then down the dorsum of my nose.

The memories echoed within the gapes of my mind,
a single teardrop dancing down the surface of my cheeks.

Make sure you sleep
I uttered,
my fingers tracing down the view of her nose
through the screen of my phone,
her face tackled by time
yet her smile remained pure.

Time does not heal.
We heal ourselves.
Time is but a hand to hold,
and the healing is our doing.
At least that's how I perceive it.
The day I am mended,
I would like to take credit for that.

The Gift of Impermanence

The youths of today
bathe in so much sadness,
their eyes becoming a dried-up river.
A haunting tragedy to know
that euphoria is a luxury
that we cannot afford.
How our young souls
weep towards the moon,
begging for pocket-sized happiness
whilst misery feasts on us
like a buffet.

Maybe in another life, we wouldn't be so sad.

Bernadette Millan

Looking back at old photos and old videos,
I fixate on
my confident ribcage
and my bulging hip-bones
that used to be visible on my 15 year old body.
It stings a bit,
looking at each image and watching *younger me*
deteriorate.

It is like watching decay creep up on a growing flower.

The Gift of Impermanence

The first time I experienced a paper-cut,
I didn't know how to react to the pain.
I didn't know whether to scream, cry
or to just wipe the blood up and go about my day.
I ended up choosing the third option.
Now, I wonder if things would have been different if I had
done the alternatives.
Because now, when trouble steers towards my direction,
it instantly goes under the rug. As if it didn't happen.
When my heart bleeds and whimper,
comfort seems to despise my presence,
and instead, I get a *"You'll get over it"* in front of a mirror.

I don't know why I've always been repulsed by the idea of
getting help.
Maybe it's because I believe that the shell I created for
myself is strong enough to carry mountains and an
abundance of affliction.
Maybe I'm just too proud, whilst I sellotape the cracks that
form within my carapace.

There is no such thing as *too much* for me.
Maybe that's why the idea of bliss is so foreign.

Bernadette Millan

My heart beats for a being that is long gone.
The silence that wreaks havoc in the mattress
that my body falls on
is covered in 5-day-old sweat stains.
It is times like this that my depression steals a piece of me,
cradling it, nursing it.
It is when my body falls submissive
to the impending weight
that will crush my healing heart
and doesn't make me shower for a week,
making my limbs heavier than I am able to lift.

The Gift of Impermanence

To my English teacher when I was in high school,

Thank you for showing me the art of literature
and how beautiful and comforting words can be.
Thank you for providing me the light that I needed
to shine a hallway full of new perspectives
and a new way to find peace within the process of writing.

Thank you Thank you Thank you Thank you Thank you
Thank you Thank you Thank you Thank you Thank you
Thank you Thank you Thank you Thank you Thank you
Thank you Thank you Thank you Thank you Thank you
Thank you Thank you Thank you Thank you Thank you
Thank you Thank you Thank you Thank you Thank you
Thank you Thank you Thank you Thank you Thank you
Thank you Thank you Thank you Thank you Thank you
Thank you Thank you Thank you Thank you Thank you
Thank you Thank you Thank you Thank you Thank you
Thank you Thank you Thank you Thank you Thank you
Thank you Thank you Thank you Thank you Thank you
Thank you Thank you Thank you Thank you Thank you
Thank you Thank you Thank you Thank you Thank you
Thank you Thank you Thank you Thank you Thank you
Thank you Thank you Thank you Thank you Thank you.

You helped save me.

Bernadette Millan

Fire.

Ignite my heart with coruscating sparks
whenever your presence is near.
Your heat warms
the cold blooded bones
and embedded bruises of my body,
relaxing the muscles
that stood tensed for what felt like a century.
The flames in your eyes
could burn into my soul with a second-long stare.
It's as if you could see right through me,
through right and wrong,
good and bad,
yet you still love me.

The Gift of Impermanence

I want you to spend
every single day with me
as if it was our last.
kiss my lips
like the sunset planted
the horizon upon my tips.
Treasure every moment
and memorise every peck.

To Mama,

You have raised three children with pure hearts.
You have given us nothing but comfort and boundless love.
You have provided warmth within days where cold would
prey on us,
and have fed our passion with support that could lift
mountains.

Inay is so proud of you.

The Gift of Impermanence

My hands felt bare,
my heart felt heavy,
my knuckles had turned white,
clothes had stuck on my frame
and night sweats acted like sellotape.

The ocean looked beautiful,
the calmness of the waves,
and the voice of the wind
is slowly luring me to take a swim.
Let me walk towards the deep end.
Let me keep walking into the horizon.

But even in the water,
everything seemed to burn.

My feet walked along the naked, translucent path,
wondering if I was able to catch up with myself.
Remembering the orbs of your eyes and its shade of deep
shallow blue,
the warmest blue my iris ever dotted on.
Your pale lips whispered me astray into the calm ocean,
the sapphire that twinkled like stars when you looked at me
brought the ladders of heaven an inch closer.
You saw me beautiful,
it made my feet stopped walking.
Weeps echoed through my hollow chest,
through my pillows,
and it made the clouds above roar as well.
My feet walked again.
And again and again and again.
The melody of your voice shamed harps and violins.
Murmuring sweet *I love you*'s that radiated through the
empty hallways that I created,
Though you added colour.
Colors such as ruby, crimson red, vermillion.
They all rested upon your cheeks,
complimented by the off-white temples that are present
when you smile.
My toes felt cold in this path. I kept walking.
No, not walking, *running*.
I run upwards, catching up with a figurine.
A figurine that is me.
It is a road to the never ending staircase of the wind
blowing petals and the clouds carrying me.
It is a road to the stars, to the moon, to the oceans above.
And I hope I see you again up here someday.

The Gift of Impermanence

Have I ever told you
how *exhausting* it is
getting you to like me?
How it disgusts me sometimes,
knowing I'd move mountains and buildings
to create a never-ending city for you.
To win the approval that I subconsciously beg
would rest on your heart and fingertips,
yet it never really was there.
I don't know if it ever really will.

The more I get you to like me,
I lose another piece of my dignity.

Sex is not just for the cause of reproduction.
Sex can be fun.
It can be exciting.
It can be *exhilarating* in fact.
Sex can make you feel good,
It can make you feel sexy.
Remember that.

I am not just an empty container
so you can fill me up and give me *meaning*.

I give myself meaning,
I give myself value.

The Gift of Impermanence

I adored her.
I adored her for the way her body
moulds into mine at night,
with the only scent that I devour hungrily
is her lavender shampoo.
I adored her for the way
she would take hours
memorising how my pupils would turn
from a deep chocolate,
to a warm pecan brown with little sepia spheres.
I adored her for how she said my name.
How her lips curled up slowly,
sounding the vowels so delicately
as if they were fragile silverware.
I adored her for all the things about her
that she hadn't ever thought of.

She is rare,
her company a blessing.
The type to make the air seem lighter,
and has an intimate relationship with internal peace.

I cannot help but adore her more and more.

Bernadette Millan

I never really had the desire to fix what we had.
I figured it would've been better to just leave.
To save any energy rather than to waste another second.
Because fixing us, *well,*
It's like screwing a new bulb on a broken lamp.

The Gift of Impermanence

I want to be a cloud.
I want to feel weightless
and have a gentle zephyr to kiss me
when the sun is absent.
And when I feel alive,
I would like to flourish a valley of flowers
that cover the Himalayas
with a gentle drizzle.
I want to cover the world
with my footsteps being disguised as raindrops.
I want to *just be.*

Bernadette Millan

I feel too much.
I wish I didn't.
It overflows and gets too heavy.
Its claws that droop the bags under my eyes,
its arms coddled my body
and tells me to stay in bed for one more day.

I wish that there was a way to rewind back time,
a way to defeat the inevitable.
Because if that was the case,
our warmth together would still be richer than pure
diamonds.

Bernadette Millan

The winter in your eyes
made me change my mind
on which season I think was
the most beautiful.
I used to say summer,
before the trail of snowflakes
left your fingertips
stopped me to a halt.
It mesmerised me.
You mesmerised me.

I'm a daydreamer.
I remain home when I picture viridescent eyes,
though the same pair never really met mine.
I like to think about the ways our hands could have
intertwined,
or how I could have made you blush.
I'm a daydreamer.
I like to picture a life with somebody
who doesn't even know I exist.

Bernadette Millan

I never imagined being jealous
of inanimate objects,
until you happened.
And now,
I need to slip underneath,
and memorise every mole, every freckle
that gets the privilege of being close to you.
Your favourite perfume submerged in luck.
What an honour it must be
to rest on the crook of your bare neck.
I need to be the pillows that you sleep on,
the coffee that you drink when you wake,
the toothpaste that you use to drown your teeth in,
the underwear that gets the pleasure of clinging onto you,
the night and day attire that gets to embrace you.
I need to be the chapstick that dances on your lips.

The Gift of Impermanence

The one thing we can do now
is to wish for better tomorrows
and hope that the future will be kinder to us.

Bernadette Millan

Thank you for hurting me.
Thank you for letting my roots grow
from the bed of thorns you threw me in.
Though you made me bleed,
you also made me realise that being with you,
is nothing better than watering a rotten flower.

The Gift of Impermanence

When tears leave their tracks across my face,
it reminds me that I am still alive.
The appearance of sorrow,
allows me to recognise that my pummelled heart still beats.
It gives me validation,
that I am still a conscious being,
despondent, yet still there.
Sometimes it is with great misery that I am thankful for.
Because without it, that's when I will realise,
that my existence is but a wandering figure,
a body with no soul.

Bernadette Millan

My soul has become ravenous,
Its empty hands need to hold onto something.
It needs love,
it needs suffering,
it sought solace within triumph,
and finds strength within failure.
It is malnourished,
It needs a meaning.

The Gift of Impermanence

In another life
maybe we become more than just a 'what if?'.
Maybe right in this moment,
our alternate selves are strolling along the esplanade,
wind wafting through our necks that are still drowning in
the perfume of each other's tongue from the night before.
Instead of my body that is sinking into this bed,
a spot next to me as bare as a blank canvas,
I would like to think that in another universe
our bodies would be so close
that the gap between us becomes a myth,
and our heartbeat becomes one.
There comes many possibilities
and outcomes when it comes to us,
however I truly believe
that my soul was supposed to love you,
and to intertwine with yours in every realities,
regardless if you would love me back.

Bernadette Millan

The Iguazu falls cry tears of joy.
A triumphing feeling it must be
to be a part of Nature's skin.

It is holy and sacred,
beautifully bare,
consisting thousands of old souls
that lurk beneath the soils.

I would love to be a part of Nature.
To be the wind that hustles through the skin of people
around town square,
the rain that pools down on cars and buildings,
marking my territory.

I would love to be
the comfort of those
who have been silenced,
and the cure for
the youth's numbness
with the kiss of my raindrops and thunderclouds.

The Gift of Impermanence

You will always be important to me
despite all of the marks and the anger.
The image of you will always sit in the every corner
of my heart and in the files of memories
that I will store forever.
Because I know that within our unsolved problems
and our shattered souls attempting to mould back together,
to fix each other,
our pieces simply did not fit.
But I know that in my heart,
we did our best
with what we were provided with at the time.

Bernadette Millan

I wonder how helpless raindrops feel,
if they were able to feel that is.
I wonder what *inevitable* feels like.
Destined to plummet down.
It could feel good, *relieving in fact,*
to know exactly what is meant to happen to my fate.
But to be surrounded by the unknown,
feels so much better.
Being on edge every time
rather than to,
well,
Settle.

Water

You entered my life
in calm waves of purity and control
as you collided with me
when I was nothing but a raging sea.
You have me drowning in the scent of your perfume,
the smell of your coffee breath
and the presence of your conditioner fragrance.
I am completely submerged under the image of you.

Bernadette Millan

Happiness is an emotion that I do not recognise.
It felt longer than forever to have peace
spread its wings across my mind,
and my heart being lighter than the whitest feather.
Is this a test?
Or is it a mocking brief stop
towards an inevitable mattress of numbness and disarray?
Is it a glimmer of light before I plunge into
a never ending darkness that my soul was meant to go in?
Don't get me wrong,
I don't mind its company.
But forgive me if I want to take precaution
to the attendance of a dove,
When my body is accustomed to vultures.

The Gift of Impermanence

The idea of you will live for eternity,
as I have you
written in the depths of my poetry.
The concept of you will blossom
from one person to another,
your eyes that peer between sentences,
and your mouth that licks through each letter
will stay embedded onto them,
and the image of you will experience decades.

Bernadette Millan

Maybe if I snapped my fingers
it will all go away.
All the constellations of trauma that my body endured
along with the obvious abandonment issues,
all of it, just, *gone*.
But it doesn't work like that does it?
It isn't that easy.
Because if it was that simple,
I would be riding down the sunset,
wearing the brightest, bluest dress,
my head being lighter than a dandelion seed by now.
But I'm not,
and that's okay.
It is alright to spend forever curing your soul,
to be able to take it one day at a time
and celebrating things like brushing your teeth.
Because *you did that.*
Despite all the invisible bruises that is submerged within
the depths of your heart
and all the painful memories that come along with it,
you were still able to tell it a big '*fuck you*',
get out of bed,
and deny it from eating you whole.
That itself,
is what I call *power.*
You don't need magic or wishful thinking,
You just need to give yourself *time.*
Time and patience.

Earth

You are what keeps me grounded.
Your skin keeps my feet down the pavement
when my head feels afloat.
You bury me deep in your heavenly scent
to the point where I have your name engraved in my veins.
Your roots seep through my core,
embedding yourself deep within me.
You keep me grounded;
you are the nature that I would forever surround myself in.

I've always wanted to go to the Grand Canyon.
Something about the way that it can influence the weather
without any external help just mesmerises me. Or how it is
a home for the hundreds, maybe even thousands, of hidden
caves makes me feel small, but in a good, comforting way.
Maybe it is also the fact that it captures the footprints of
many different people across the world, and carries
centuries within its flesh. It is an ancient, yet refreshing
landscape. It would be an honour to be within its company.

Time can be ruthless. Your depression could be eating you bit by bit, sucking the life out of you, however the clock won't stop ticking. Time does not wait for you to get better. There will be things that come up or occasions that surface. There will be new tomorrows and many more nights. Seasons will also come and go. Birthdays happen and Halloweens, maybe even Christmases. Circumstances will always be changing regardless of how you feel or don't feel. But what you need to remember is that despite you feeling as though you are trailing behind, *time is not your enemy*. Time does not want you to fail nor does it create possibilities for further sorrow. Time simply gives us keys to enter doors within our future. The future that we want for ourselves. It is good to be patient. Don't worry, nobody is rushing you. And when you are ready, time has a way of directing you into a new day, a new beginning, a new key. And whatever happens next, that is for you to decide.

- *So please, don't rush your healing process.*

Bernadette Millan

Sometimes the only thing you really need is the sympathy
of Mother Nature.
On the nights where your weeping becomes unbearable,
she would command the sky and the clouds
to drown them out with a passionate thunderclap.
And if that's not what you need,
she would present the brightest glow within the stars,
intense enough to wrestle the darkness that circles you.
Or the days where you feel inadequate,
she would beam the golden sun to glaze over your skin
and reflect the ocean within your eyes,
just to show how utterly beautiful you are.
And if you want something else,
she would form an everlasting rain
and cry with you
to help take away that lonesome feeling.

The Gift of Impermanence

For my healing soul,

I forgive you
for abusing our body.
I know skipping that meal
seemed the perfect solution
to feel good enough.
I forgive you
for smoking that first cigarette
not long after your first period
because you didn't want to be left behind.
I forgive you
for bruising our body
because I understand that by doing so,
felt much better, rather than to feel nothing at all.
I forgive you
for wanting the attention of those older men,
because despite it not ending well,
I know that it made you feel good,
made you feel seen for once.
I forgive you.
Now *please*,
for the love of God,
Heal for me.

Bernadette Millan

Art has a way of being an advocate
for our vulnerable souls.
Art provides a voice
within the mouths that were silenced.
Art becomes a friend,
a therapist,
a warm embrace.
Art takes the pain away,
and turns it into something *beautiful*.

The Gift of Impermanence

There is this hill that I have always loved going to every
year since I was 8 years old.
I don't know why but it's one of the things that I look
forward to the most.
It's something about watching the surrounding trees and
cobblestones differ within each visit,
watching the world age with me.
It provides me calmness to know that it is not just me
that's maturing,
but that everything is ever-changing.
It is the gift of impermanence.
And I suppose that may be deemed as frightening,
but within the depths of the fear
there is also beauty within it.
That nothing really is concrete,
with change being the only thing that is immortal.

I've come to accept that not everyone will like you.
Not everyone will see the good parts,
or will allow themselves to *see* the good parts.
Not everyone will understand your pain,
your healing, your trauma, *you*.
People will talk,
some people will be so mean,
but don't let them devour you.

You are golden.

The Gift of Impermanence

It is with great pleasure
to tell you that the sadness
will soon fade.
You will be able to breathe again,
and be able to do the things you once loved.
You will be able to find joy in the tiniest littlest things,
and you will find new things that will bring you
contentment.
This is not a forever,
this misery is not permanent,
it is but a pit-stop
towards an infinite party of new beginnings
and happy endings.

Bernadette Millan

Growth is eternal,
never settle for anything less.

Acknowledgements

This poetry collection would not have been put out there without the help and encouragement of so many people.

I want to thank each and every one of you for allowing me to blossom and grow into the person that I am.

Firstly thank you to the many organisations that provide help towards those who are struggling mentally such as Samaritans and Mind. Even just to listen to those voices that had felt neglect. It really does goes a long way.

Thank you to my family, especially my mum. Thank you for encouraging me to write down my feelings and, in a way, turn them into something less 'unpleasant'. Thank you for teaching me acceptance of the good, the bad, and everything else in between. Thank you for inspiring some of these poems and for being my rock.

Thank you to Ysabelle Jao for taking the time and doing my illustrations and turning my words into something visual. Your concepts with the pieces had me in awe.

To my former teacher Mrs. Constable, thank you for being a part of my healing journey and for being a catalyst for my love towards English literature in the early days. You made high school more bearable, and your comfort is something that I will treasure forever.

To Chloe, thank you from the bottom of my heart. Thank you for helping me and encouraging me to share my writing further than in my bedroom, staying silent on my notes. Thank you for staying patient, thank you for being my person.

To Aimee and Kiran, I absolutely adore you both and thank you for all the support that you have given me. I hope that you two liked some of these poems that each of you have been an inspiration for.

To Zenne, there are no words to describe how grateful I am to have met you. Thank you for staying and sticking through every obstacle and for showing me nothing but kindness. You showed me that there are genuine goodness in this world, and for that, I thank you.

To one of my longest and dearest friend Beth, I love you. Thank you for showing me all the wrong and the good throughout our high school years, for giving me tough love (and knocking some sense into me at times when I've needed!). Thank you for staying all these years.

To Hannah, what can I say?! Without your kind words and your moral support throughout our university degree course, I would've been in a ball of tears most nights. Thank you, thank you, thank you!!

Lastly, thank you to all of my other friends and family, I love every single one of you. Thank you for not abandoning, especially on times when I needed comfort the most. *Mahal ko kayong lahat.*

Printed in Great Britain
by Amazon